MEMORIES OF HOME

MEMORIES OF HOME

HEIDI CAILLIER

INTERIORS

PHOTOGRAPHY BY HARIS KENJAR | FOREWORD BY AMBER LEWIS

RIZZOLI
NEW YORK

New York · Paris · London · Milan

For Rowan and Soter

CONTENTS

FOREWORD

Here's what I love about Heidi: She has a way of incorporating patterns, using big chintzes and plaids, that's so unique. Her work is traditional, but it's also eclectic. Her style is timeless and fresh, both tailored and extremely playful. I know from experience that designing like this isn't an easy task, yet she makes it look effortless. Simply put, she has incredible taste.

Every time H'eidi posts a photo of one of her projects on Instagram, I wonder, "Is this new? Or has it been there forever?" That's intended as a true compliment. Creating work that feels both classic and of the moment is an achievement.

Like many of you, I discovered Heidi's work on Instagram, where we developed a modern "e-lationship." We comment on each other's photos and support each other in that online world. The design community is surprisingly close that way. Later, I realized that we both started out as bloggers, and while it's been fun to watch many people from that time experience success, it's been especially delightful to see Heidi get the recognition she deserves.

Another thing I love about Heidi, which people discover when they follow her on social media, is that she is outspoken and confident. You understand immediately that she doesn't care what people think. There's an edginess to her personality and her work that I really appreciate. She has conviction about her point of view, and she wants to stay as authentic as possible, to be the same person from one year to the next. She's fearless and real, and that is rare in our world.

At this point, everyone has seen that photo of her green kitchen with the hexagonal terracotta tile floor on some corner of the Internet. I always come back to it, and it always feels current. By now, it's an iconic image. Heidi's photos, and her aesthetic, are so recognizable to so many interior design lovers that my hope is she soon becomes a household name.

My prediction is that it's only a matter of time.

—Amber Lewis

INTRODUCTION

Some people are born with a creative calling and a distinct sense of purpose, and they work toward their goals with commitment and clear direction. This has always been particularly true in the world of interior design. Many designers talk about their childhood homes, and their mother's collections, and their memories of beautiful rooms filled with family heirlooms, passed down through generations. Rearranging the furniture in their bedrooms for as long as they can remember.

I was not one of those people.

In my younger years, I did not have the luxury of this clear focus. What I did have was a sense of adventure, and a desire to accumulate experiences and knowledge. I was passionate—I just didn't know about what.

As a student, I thought I wanted to become a doctor, or work in the public health sector. I got a degree in sociology and women's studies and then went straight to graduate school for a master's degree in international public health. I worked in Africa and came back to the United States to look for equally fulfilling and meaningful work. What I found were jobs that were largely administrative, and a little dull. I didn't know exactly what I was looking for, but I knew it wasn't a life behind a desk. I spent many years after that adding to the list of things I didn't want to do—acupuncture school, nursing school, accounting school. I tended bar. I waited tables. I was a scuba instructor in Australia. I studied yoga in India. It was a full and interesting life, but nothing clicked for me career-wise. None of it felt exactly right.

Growing up, I never lived anywhere for longer than three years before I finished high school. My father was in the army, and after that he became a Baptist minister, so we moved all the time.

I was born in Japan. Subsequently, I lived in Virginia, Washington, D.C., Wisconsin, South Dakota, Massachusetts, New York, New Orleans, San Francisco, and now the Pacific Northwest. I have flashes of memories from all of the houses I lived in, but I didn't have a profound, deep connection with any one home. I now understand that part of my desire to create homes for others is rooted in this experience—as an adult, I can see how it influenced me, and why I do what I do.

After I moved to San Francisco from New Orleans, I found myself drawn into the world of interiors and started a design blog. I wrote that faithfully for a brief period of a few years before realizing that I would rather be designing homes than talking about designing homes. It was then that I landed my first design job.

There is a misconception that interior design is a casually paced, light job that involves browsing through textile libraries and picking out furnishings. Nothing is further from the truth. There is an incredible amount of technical knowledge required for this job, and the number of details that must be considered is immense. This profession is not just walking into a store and picking out a sofa, and they do not teach you most of what you need to know on a day-to-day level in design school. You learn it on the job through trial and error.

I worked for two designers before I went out on my own. At first, I said yes to every job. Starting out can be tough, creatively. Because you want to make your clients happy (and you are often working with very limited budgets), you're doing exactly what people tell you they want. It felt predictable and uninspired. After a few years of working this way, I started to realize that I had no idea who I was as a designer. I took a pause to look more closely at what I was doing, and to figure out why it didn't line up with what I loved. This helped me figure out what I want to put out into the world. When I stopped doing what I thought people expected of me and started doing what I wanted to do, it all clicked.

What I discovered is a love of tension—a play between masculine and feminine, old and new, modern and traditional. I don't like to use the word pretty to describe my work. I want it to feel unexpected, but rooted in tradition, and also layered and eclectic. I found that mixing patterns, combining florals with graphic lines and shapes, and using deeper, muddy colors connected me with my work—and, in turn, connected others with it as well. When you believe strongly in your vision, people will respond. This conviction has served me well, and I still encourage clients to go all the way with the process. Those who are the happiest with their homes are the clients who trust me and my team enough to let the visions come to life.

Running and growing my business has required a tremendous amount of hard work. When I see the collection of photos in the pages of this book, however, the long hours and challenges fade into the background. All I feel is gratitude. It's a privilege to do this work.

My life has been a bit unconventional, it's true, but all of my unusual, disconnected experiences have fed my imagination. That's where inspiration comes from. You don't have to have memories of a storybook house to create one. My hope is that the collection of houses I've assembled for this book provides ample proof that that sentiment is true.

Scattered across the country, from the bucolic suburbs of New York to the shores of Tacoma, the city I now call home, these are my most cherished projects to date. The photos and words weave together to tell a story that is nostalgic, romantic, creative, playful but sophisticated, and so incredibly comforting. I hope those feelings emanate from these pages. My journey as a designer and a person is far from over, but when I look back at these homes I helped bring to life, it feels like a path well-traveled thus far.

BERKELEY HILLS

The intention for this three-story 1920s Bay Area Craftsman was to preserve as many of the original details as possible. The young owners consider themselves stewards and caretakers of this property. They wanted to respect the architecture of this redwood-shingle-clad house in a neighborhood where early Berkeleyans could sit on their porches and observe the construction of the first buildings that created the San Francisco skyline. They hired the same contractors who had worked on the house for years and were very conscientious about making interior alterations that felt authentic to the house.

The couple has a deliberate, intentional lifestyle that I admire. As a child, the wife bounced between the French countryside and the vibrant Berkeley food scene, and that experience informed how she and her husband wanted to live and raise their own family. They really abide by the tenets of "slow living," and love to work in the garden and make gorgeous meals together. The property, with its large terraced hillside garden, feels like it's from an era when this lifestyle was more common. I couldn't imagine a more perfect home for them.

The front entrance is accessed by a series of stone steps, and the home is surrounded by a curtain of thick, green bamboo. It's like a private retreat nestled in the treetops, but it's so close to the city, you can see the bay from the top-floor windows and each tier of the garden.

Bamboo and large windows bring the outside in.

PREVIOUS SPREAD: A tiled pink fireplace surround and woven pendant shade keep the living room young. ABOVE: The listening room, for lounging or playing records. OPPOSITE: An Indian dhurrie and an Audoux Minet console add to the collected feel.

OPPOSITE: Linen on the walls softens the contrast with the original dark wood. ABOVE: Woven Indian blinds filter the light.

PREVIOUS SPREAD: The dining chairs' brick-hued linen complements the soft blush ceiling. ABOVE: Using the same floral for wallpaper, lamp shade, and pillows creates a subtle monoprint room. OPPOSITE: A petite French marble sink fits this powder room perfectly.

Just inside the front door, there's a nook with tall, multi-paned windows and built-in daybeds. It's a spot for morning coffee, and to prepare for the day ahead. The main living area is divided into a sitting room in front of the fireplace and a listening room with a built-in bench we designed to mimic existing millwork. This is where they play records and enjoy the dappled sunlight that makes this property so special.

When we were discussing influences, they mentioned they were drawn to the quirky style of young British designers, who are great at combining vibrant color with cozy elements and a traditional European countryside aesthetic, and we all agreed that we wanted to put a new spin on some classic ideas. The glossy pink tile around the fireplace was one of the ways we made the dark-paneled room more youthful and fun. Instead of a serious Arts and Crafts light fixture, we installed a simple pendant light with a wicker shade. The denim-blue rug is an antique Indian dhurrie, and the mix of textiles is eclectic but harmonious.

Working with the dark wood tones of a Craftsman can be tricky. I find the contrast between the deep stain and white paint to be too stark. To make it a little less severe, we covered the frieze area above the paneling in linen. The ceiling in the dining room, between the beams, is painted blush pink for the same reason.

I found a couple of spectacular vintage pieces before I even had a chance to make a full presentation to the owners. I always want a house to feel like it was decorated with a mix of family heirlooms and inherited furniture, and unique vintage accents lend authenticity. But once they're sold, they're gone forever. To the clients' credit, they trusted me enough to let me procure the items based on

A new built-in mimics the original millwork.

RIGHT: An elongated kitchen island with rounded edges provides generous space for meal prep.
FOLLOWING PAGES: Kitchen details: warm copper counters and vintage tiles.

PREVIOUS SPREAD AND OPPOSITE: We embraced the flood of natural light on the upper floor with an airy palette in the primary bedroom. ABOVE: Curtained French doors hide an office nook.

photos alone, so I could acquire them before they were gone. The pomegranate ceramic lamp on the Audoux Minet console is a favorite and was a fantastic find. The hanging pendant light with the ruffled shade in the listening room was another. And the petite marble sink in the pocket-size powder room was an absolute must. It fits snugly in the corner, and is paired with a sweet block print pattern on the walls and the shade. A casual backsplash that looks like it might have been cobbled together from leftover tile dresses down the ornate sink.

The blue-and-white porcelain chandelier over the dining table actually is a family heirloom, and it works so beautifully in this room with the rush-backed dining chairs upholstered in a rich rose-toned linen.

In the kitchen, a mix of vintage tiles creates a backsplash behind the workspace and the Lacanche range. Copper counters add a bit of reflective glow, while an island found in England contributes modern functionality.

The family bedrooms and bathrooms, a small office, and a garden room are all upstairs. Because the first floor leans dark, the owners wanted the second floor to be airy and light. We kept the existing shutters, and chose some very pretty, feminine textiles, like a vintage quilt for the bed and an antique kilim rug in the principal bedroom. The second-floor hallway is papered in a John Derian print—a stunning floral that feels both charming and modern. The garden room gets beautiful light and is surrounded on three sides by stunning views of the outdoors. There's a casual sitting area and a game table in the corner. It really is a lovely place to play a game of backgammon or curl up and read a book, and, like the rest of this unique and thoughtful home, it's very reflective of the people who inhabit it.

PREVIOUS PAGES: A delicate floral paper on the landing leads to a sweet nursery.
OPPOSITE: Seagrass, rattan, and leafy green bring the outside in.

BEDFORD

One of the few positive outcomes from the pandemic is that everyone has grown more comfortable working on projects remotely. When the owners of this home in Bedford, New York, a traditional bedroom community northeast of Manhattan, contacted me, I had never taken on a job from such a distance. Things have changed dramatically in a short time, and now the majority of my work is outside of the Pacific Northwest.

The clients are a young family who were moving out of the city. They were looking for some light renovation work and furnishings. I was very excited by the idea of working on this quintessential East Coast house. I lived on the East Coast for a portion of my young life and really respond to these eighteenth-century homes with character. You just don't encounter houses like this in the West. The original structure was built in 1790, and it has the thick beams, double-sided fireplace, and snug proportions that are typical of that era. The house had been expanded with an addition some years ago, but overall, it maintained many of its original architectural details.

Because of the home's historic provenance, we felt like we could have fun with some more traditional decorative elements, like the collection of beautiful plates hung on the wall of the breakfast nook, the de Gournay wallpaper in the dining room, and some bold floral textiles. These are all nods to the history of the structure, and add a collected feel to the interiors that's intentional. This house, with its oversized fireplaces, small-scale rooms, and awkwardly placed beams, is a bit too quirky to be straightforwardly formal, so we wanted to incorporate some playfulness. In the living room we installed half-height cafe curtains, added an African Tuareg rug made from reed and leather and an unexpected mix of

The furnishings in the rich blue family room reflect the traditional yet unconventional mix of the house.

RIGHT: Plaid and botanicals mingle happily. An antique oil painting is balanced by the contemporary Moroccan rug and organic wood table. FOLLOWING SPREAD: The odd angles and exposed beams of the kitchen reveal where the original structure ends and the new additions begin. OVERLEAF: Clever storage in the small breakfast nook is built around a window, allowing for plenty of natural light.

PREVIOUS SPREAD AND OPPOSITE: Large floral patterns, like the linen on this proper tufted upholstered sofa, are elegant without being overly serious. ABOVE AND FOLLOWING SPREAD: Feminine, hand-painted de Gournay wallpaper is grounded by plaid dining chairs with scallop-edged skirts.

patterned pillows on the sofa, and placed an oddly beautiful ceramic Baobab lamp from Porta Romana on a side table. I like every room to have something just a little weird, or off. It often makes the whole room.

To keep the design rooted in the present day, we balanced classic elements with a more modern globe light fixture, a large-scale photograph by Tania Franco Klein in the living room, and dining chairs upholstered in a masculine plaid that have ladylike scalloped skirts. I love the tension of handsome versus pretty in these chairs.

The newer rooms of the home, including the family room and the primary bedroom, were built with higher vaulted ceilings. To make the family room feel cozier, we painted the walls and ceiling a deep ocean blue. In the bedroom, we made the large space feel more intimate by playing with a soft pattern on the walls and repeating it on the lampshades and pillows.

There is a lovely snug kids' bedroom on the second floor, tucked under the eaves, that is part of the original house. We hung antique paintings on the wall, used furnishings that convey the feel of the era, and covered the twin beds in vintage flour-sack quilts. When you see the room, you get the feeling that it could have been there—looking exactly that way—for many years.

Once the house was finished and photographed, the most surprising reward came in the form of a message I received out of the blue. A woman saw pictures of this house and recognized it as her childhood home, which her parents owned for almost forty years. She felt such a connection to the work we did that she wanted us to design a new home she'd purchased on Nantucket. It was nice to know that the house felt fresh but authentic, as if we were shepherding it through its third century in a thoughtful, considered way.

PREVIOUS SPREAD: The bedrooms are muted, peaceful, and grounded in earth tones.
RIGHT: A charming attic bedroom with angular nooks, twin spindle beds, and vintage quilts.

NORTH END

This home is where I live with my husband, our sons, and our beloved dog. You can learn a lot about a designer from their personal space, and this house feels like me, and my family, in every way.

Our Tudor is in North Tacoma, a charming, historic neighborhood in Tacoma, Washington, with views of the sound. We had been looking in the area for several years and knew as soon as we walked in that this would be our next home. The layout was quite nice as it was and, while the house needed aesthetic updates, I was sure we could make it very special without having to take down significant walls or add square footage. The views were lovely, and there was a sense of expansiveness that neither of us had experienced in years.

While the location is what attracted us to the property, we ultimately fell in love with the bones of the house. I have an affinity for old properties, and I was drawn to the dramatic pitch of the roofline, the original windows, and the pretty architectural elements. Aside from expanding the kitchen a bit and adding a bathroom off of my sons' bedroom, we left the layout as it was. We kept all of the original doors, windows, and trim, and renovated the kitchen, bathrooms, and lighting throughout. I wanted to respect the architecture and style of the home and considered that heavily when designing the interiors.

My husband is an avid cook, and, like many families, we spend a lot of time in our kitchen. The layout was tricky because it is not huge, but it is very functional for us. A kitchen nook is a great way to create more seating in a small space, and after I built this one in my own kitchen it became a staple in the homes I design. My affinity for natural materials led me to soapstone for the counters, and I love this shade of green paint, which functions like a warm neutral.

I love a nook, like this one in our kitchen. You can only take a room so far with furniture.

To honor the classic Tudor architecture of our home,
I made the interiors formal but still family-friendly.

PREVIOUS SPREAD: The custom millwork in the living room, painted a traditional blue, lets the television recede into the background. LEFT: The antique French chandelier was one of the first pieces I purchased for our home. Windsor-style chairs and a simple striped rug combine to create a comfortable, classic dining room.

OPPOSITE AND ABOVE: Soft gray soapstone countertops pair well with the terracotta floors, gray-green paint, and brass hardware.

A traditional lantern pendant in the nook and simple wood pendants over the island create layered lighting in the kitchen.

We removed a butler's door that connected the kitchen to the dining room and replaced it with an archway to create a better flow and a sense of openness between the rooms. The mid-century French chandelier was the very first thing I bought. It is perfectly quirky and classic at the same time. It set a tone for what I wanted the rest of the interiors to look like.

The living room is right off of the entry and needed to set the tone. The Calacatta Verde marble surround on the fireplace is always the first thing people comment on. I searched for months for the perfect bold floral fabric for the chair and ottoman. I knew I had found the right one in this special Jean Monro textile. The tramp-art mirror over the fireplace is another special piece I found early on. I bought it without knowing where it would go, but I'm a firm believer that if you love something, you will find a place for it. It ended up working perfectly over the fireplace. The bit of Oval Room Blue from Farrow & Ball on the millwork adds depth and brings some richness to a room with white walls. There's a second, more casual living area off the kitchen that we call the toy room. It's darker, cozier—a kind of snug—and it's where we spend a lot of family time. It's where the boys play, and where my husband and I often watch a movie at night.

Our bedroom is arguably my favorite room in the house. Doing a bedroom in soft pink is always a good idea. It is a warm and inviting color that cocoons you. I love a monoprint, meaning one pattern that is used in multiple ways throughout a room, and had long coveted a room like this. The upholstered walls glow at night when there's a lamp on, and again in the morning when the warm sunlight comes in.

There are three bedrooms on the second floor: the primary bedroom, one for guests, and one that the boys share. We ask them on occasion if they'd like their own rooms, and the answer is always a resounding no. Everything I've chosen for this room, including the Swedish rag rugs that I had stitched together to make a larger area rug, reads elegant, but in a young way. They'll grow into the room, like we've grown into the rest of the house. I hope we stay here forever.

The powder room is painted a muted lavender. A floral sconce—one of a pair—and a freestanding vanity make this room feel like it has been here forever.

ABOVE: Whenever I find something I love, I add to the gallery wall of vintage oil paintings and artwork. The deep navy walls make the small room snug and welcoming. OPPOSITE: This dark and cozy area off the kitchen is where our sons play.

PREVIOUS SPREAD: Upholstered soft pink walls in the primary bedroom are enveloping. ABOVE AND OPPOSITE: Indigo accents keep the room from reading monochrome. Using the same fabric for the walls, headboard, drapery, and lampshades creates a cocoon-like atmosphere.

PREVIOUS PAGE, LEFT: Floral wallpaper with a subtle sheen lines the walls of the entry and stairwell. PREVIOUS PAGE, RIGHT: The tile pattern on the primary bathroom floor is fresh but rooted in tradition. RIGHT: The neutral palette in our guest bedroom.

ABOVE AND OPPOSITE: Our twin sons love sharing a room furnished with a pair of single four-poster beds.

PITTSFIELD

Built in 1940 and situated on a lush six-acre lot, this colonial in the Berkshires is as graceful and interesting as its owners. Design-lovers and West Coast transplants, they wanted to honor the traditional bones and pedigree of the property by choosing furnishings that reflect the elegant architecture and adding a few formal details like archways and moldings. There are enough unexpected and eclectic details woven throughout to keep the house from feeling staid.

When you enter the front door, you'll find a striped slipper chair trimmed in aubergine fringe situated next to a sweeping banister. It's elegant and irreverent. The use of a small-print wallpaper in many of the home's common spaces—including the vestibule, the hallways, and the stairwell—brings charm to often overlooked areas. I like to work with monochromatic pattern, like this warm gray, because it doesn't overwhelm, even when it appears on large surfaces like wallpaper or fabric for drapery. Using this paper liberally, even near the back entrance, creates a beautiful flow—and that comforting, cocooned sensation—throughout.

In the living room, the BDDW sofa would be a work of art even with the simplest upholstery fabric, but a bold green chintz print takes it to a new level. This is one of my favorite statement sofas and it sings in this room. The pistachio green

This classic property in the Berkshires has elegantly proportioned rooms updated with custom molding, coffered paneling, and graceful archways.

RIGHT: The artwork is a puzzle from Tyler Hays's Bather
series. The modern sofa shape is given a traditional
spin with chintz. FOLLOWING SPREAD: We used a mix of
patterns in this formal living room.

PREVIOUS SPREAD AND LEFT: A built-in bench with a French tufted cushion provides seating for the table while allowing space for people to travel through the dining room, which is open on three sides. We commissioned a custom mural with flora and fauna native to the Berkshires.

on the walls reads very neutral and is a more nuanced alternative to white walls. We covered the floor with a thick, woven grass rug to keep the room from becoming too precious. From the petite daybed to the detailed woodwork, there isn't a corner of this room that isn't considered.

Originally, the living and dining areas were one large room. We separated them by adding an archway to create a dining nook and built a long banquette under the windows for seating on one side of the table. The custom mural by James Mobley, a completely one-of-a-kind installation reflecting the surrounding Berkshires, brings in a personal touch.

We wanted to create a home in which every room holds a mix of serious furniture and playful touches. In the powder room, an antique marble sink and traditional mural play nicely with a vintage rattan mirror, painted checkerboard floors, and a green mid-century sconce. The lady's office has a vintage French ceiling light that is countered by mismatched chairs in coordinating upholstery and a collection of flea-market floral oils that the owners will add to over time.

In the kitchen, to add warmth and soften the reclaimed limestone tile floor and the white marble topping the island, we used wood for the countertops. The cabinets in the main area are painted in a putty-colored neutral and those in the butler's pantry in a high-gloss celadon.

The open layout calls for a cohesive palette and furnishings.

PREVIOUS SPREAD: Reclaimed limestone covers the floor of the kitchen. OPPOSITE AND ABOVE: A butler's pantry pairs celery green and warm brass. The artwork is a piece painted by the client's mother.

OPPOSITE: The bathroom feels playful; an antique marble sink mixes with a French rattan mirror and mid-century sconce.
ABOVE: A small-scale floral print wallpaper covers most hallway and common area walls.

RIGHT: In the game room, ticking stripe curtains, olive-toned walls, and a cozy lilac sectional make this corner an ideal spot to watch a movie. FOLLOWING SPREAD: An adjacent game table and wet bar.

OPPOSITE: A wood vanity and graphic floor tile in the son's bathroom. ABOVE: The daughter's bathroom with its skirted sink, delicate painting, and brass sconces.

PREVIOUS SPREAD: Four patterns mingle in the primary bedroom. ABOVE AND OPPOSITE: The bedroom features a Swedish armoire and Thonet bentwood chair.

Varying marble tiles were painstakingly selected to create a one-of-a-kind mosaic in the primary bathroom. Smoky lavender millwork warms the room, while vintage brass shield mirrors, mid-century sconces, and a ladylike club chair make it eclectic and inviting.

Off of the dining room, there's a large game room with a pool table and a bar—the ideal spot for entertaining. A rattan pendant hangs over a card table with comfortable loungy chairs. A lavender-striped upholstered sectional is a cozy spot to gather and watch a movie and is offset by modern artwork.

Upstairs, the son's bathroom is finished in glossy blue tile paired with a dark wood vanity and graphic stone flooring that has a masculine edge. The daughter's bathroom has a sweet skirted sink and a tiny, family heirloom painting on the wall. The primary bath feels like a sanctuary, with its reeded wood vanity, smoky lilac walls, and a one-of-a-kind floor that we designed by selecting a variety of colorful stone tiles.

The primary bedroom is both elegant and comfortable, with its muted rug woven with soft lavender tones and upholstered walls. Fabric on the walls adds warmth to a bedroom and conveys the exact feeling you want to experience when you're getting ready for bed. The nightstands are painted pot cupboards from England, and I love the contrast of the rustic Swedish armoire with the clean lines of a mid-century Thonet chair.

Working on this home was a joyful process from conception to finish, and there's evidence of that everywhere you look.

OPPOSITE: An archway creates a dedicated nook for a freestanding tub.
FOLLOWING PAGES: A collection of vintage floral oil paintings in the home office; mismatched chairs are unified by blue-and-white striped fabric.

SEWARD PARK

Some design styles and eras are more difficult to mix and match than others, like mid-century modern and East Coast traditional. It's challenging but not impossible, and this house in the Seward Park neighborhood in southeast Seattle, across Lake Washington from Mercer Island, is a great example of how they can work together. The bones of the home are modern, but the couple who owned it had different ideas about how to furnish it. She wanted the clean lines of Danish design, and he had more classic taste. So, after we gutted the house for a full interior remodel, we put it back together in a way that blended the two styles. We added some unexpected moments of color and some playful textiles to stitch the two aesthetics together, and I think you can really see the harmony between the two worlds.

In the living and dining room, the coffered wall panels, fireplace mantel, and trim are classic in design, but the terracotta paint gives it all a contemporary spin. The sofa is upholstered in a bold floral print, and its simple lines are juxtaposed with the softer form of the skirted armchair that sits across from it. A contemporary painting hangs between two scalloped brass sconces on the wall. The round dining table, walnut armchairs, and credenza have a 1960s vintage spirit, but plaid upholstery and teal paint add warmth and rusticity to their clean lines. Rush-seat chairs, wicker, and rattan pieces throughout the house bridge the gap between classic Americana and modernism.

The kitchen was the subject of much discussion. My clients knew that most of their meals would be eaten at the island, so they wanted enough counter stools for everyone in the family. Instead of building a breakfast nook, which was my

OPPOSITE AND FOLLOWING SPREAD: Warm colors and rich textures give these Danish chairs and credenza a fresh perspective.

A jute rug grounds the bold
botanical print sofa. The painting
is flanked by playful sconces.

RIGHT: The family enjoys sharing meals at the generous island. FOLLOWING PAGES: This kitchen gets its warmth from brass fixtures, Arabescato countertops, handmade tile, and soft green on the cabinetry.

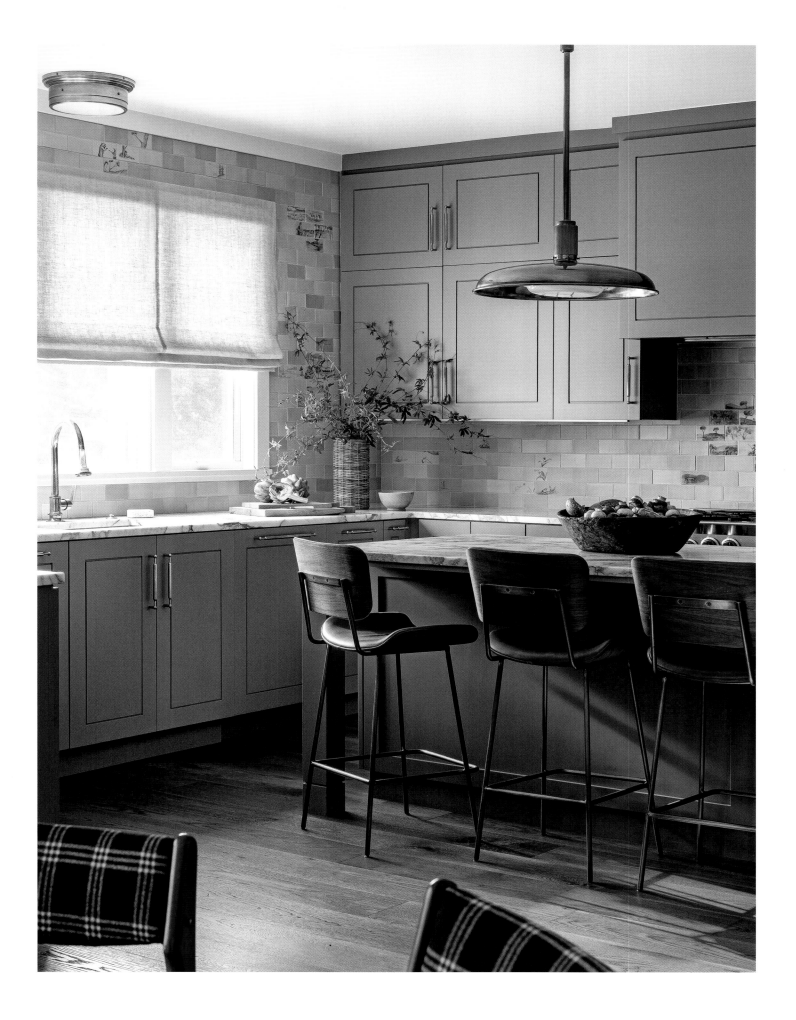

initial instinct, we created a small built-in lounge area where the kids sit and have snacks and watch their shows on a small television we built into the side of the island. I love the brass pendants in the kitchen, which marry a modern look with a more classic finish.

We played with some fun patterns in the kids' bedrooms, including a large-scale woodland animal print in one bedroom that is beautiful and adventurous at the same time, and sailboat pattern draperies that won't feel babyish or dated as the children get older.

The primary bedroom leans more modern. I typically like to use two levels of lighting on a nightstand, a sconce and a lamp—one for reading and the other for more ambient light. This was the first and only time I used pendant lights rather than sconces. They really work with the modern caned headboard. But the room comes back around to a more traditional feel with the Kotan fabric used for the curtains and the gingham upholstered chair.

We found a beautiful slab of Calacatta Viola marble to use in the primary bathroom, and I love the drama of it. It's glamorous, with a chic 1970s vibe. I like a richly patterned marble. It's a welcome departure from Carrara that has become ubiquitous. We used it to full effect in this room.

Every space in this house was well-considered, including a daylight basement playroom for the children that has doors that open to the outside and is covered in a beautiful but irreverent wallpaper featuring majestic looking birds. Even the mudroom/office has thoughtful built-ins and a little adjacent powder room that feels like a surprise with its lovely tile detail.

A built-in nook at the far end of the kitchen is a spot for afterschool snacks and morning coffee.

A mudroom that also functions as a home office. Built-in storage along the wall conceals coats and backpacks.

ABOVE: A Papa Bear chair in saffron yellow is a restful spot to curl up with a book. OPPOSITE: A playroom is a fun area for experimenting with bold pattern. FOLLOWING SPREAD AND OVERLEAF PAGES: In the primary bedroom, we kept the palette simple but used a combination of textures: nubby grass cloth on the walls, a wicker headboard, and soft carpeting.

Bold marble counteracts the sweetness of the floor tiles in this primary bathroom.

ABOVE: A palette of deep indigo, forest and sage greens, and sunny yellow is grounded by neutral grass-cloth walls.
OPPOSITE AND FOLLOWING PAGES: Playful but refined patterns help kids' bedrooms grow with them as they age.

FOX ISLAND

My involvement with the owners of this graceful home on Fox Island began with a brief phone call and we quickly discovered synergy. The clients wanted to create elegant interiors with plenty of dramatic pattern and custom details. They were drawn to richer wood tones, like walnut, and bold, graphic, untraditional patterns.

The house was a new build on Fox Island, which is near Gig Harbor, over the Narrows Bridge from Tacoma, Washington. The land was gorgeous, and the view was breathtaking. I came onto the project after the architectural plans had been drawn, just in time to make a few additions and changes.

The scale of the rooms was quite large. Most of the rooms had ten-foot ceilings—the great room's even more capacious. Originally, the clients were focused on avoiding anything that felt trendy. They wanted statement-making seating, distinguished vintage pieces, and cozy textiles, but furnishings alone can't make a room. Architectural elements like wood paneling, millwork, and wallpaper are necessary, especially in large-scale, new houses, which can lack character. I drew up plans for an efficient desk and work nook in their son's room, shelving for their large collection of books in an office, and the cane-front piece in the great room. Once they saw the design, they understood how it would help make the rooms feel intimate.

OPPOSITE: A sofa in moss-green wool and draperies in a small-scale print occupy a corner of the primary bedroom suite. FOLLOWING PAGES: A stone fireplace is the focal point of the great room. We balanced the warmth of the stone with cool blue-gray walls.

ABOVE: A richly veined marble makes a statement. OPPOSITE: The dining area is grounded with an antique kilim rug and live-edge wood table.

RIGHT: High ceilings in the kitchen translate to plenty of cabinet space. The dark millwork brings depth to a room that is flooded with natural light.

ABOVE AND OPPOSITE: Natural colors and textures in the office. FOLLOWING SPREAD: The Togo sofa in a blue batik textile reflects the clients' adventurous spirit.

To find a shared aesthetic, the clients and I sent ideas and images back and forth. I could see that they were drawn to dark colors and black hardware, and our styles didn't seem aligned. It took some time, but we worked together to determine what they loved, helping them distill their vision. We found common aesthetic ground in our mutual love for mid-century design, with all of us preferring the curvier lines in French and Italian furniture from that era over American counterparts.

The house has a layered, collected feel. Linen and grass-cloth wallcoverings and custom-made pieces mix with plenty of vintage finds (some of my all-time favorite pieces live in this house). To me, the most memorable piece of furniture in this home, and the one that's received the most attention, is the vintage Togo sofa in the media room. Initially, I wanted this room to be monoprint—the sofa, walls, and curtains all clad in the same pattern. The clients weren't as excited about this idea, but eventually we arrived at a compromise in the form of this low-slung, modern, iconic sofa shape in a contrasting indigo botanical print textile. It is a great example of how important it is to be confident in what you like; these owners have an adventurous approach to pattern and design. It also demonstrates how bold florals don't always read as feminine.

The challenge with a new home is to make it feel like it's been there for generations, and will stand for generations to come, and I feel like, together, we achieved that goal with this home.

PREVIOUS SPREAD: The primary suite is more reserved, with walls and a custom bedframe upholstered in peachy neutrals. OPPOSITE: A seating area in the primary suite with a modern wingback chair and textiles in soft brown and olive green.

OPPOSITE: Bookshelves line the walls of a workspace and library.
ABOVE: A caned vanity is a strong counterpart to graphic wallpaper.

PREVIOUS PAGES: A built-in desk and bookshelf in a boy's room. ABOVE: Deep olive grass cloth and a Noguchi lantern add texture to a son's bedroom. OPPOSITE: A kids' bathroom has contrasting tiles.

A guest room incorporates a blue plaid headboard and a pair of mid-century chairs, in their original upholstery, against a backdrop of muted salmon.

OPPOSITE: Glossy aubergine walls and chambray-blue penny tile floors pair with a wood vanity and modern lighting. FOLLOWING SPREAD: A girl's bedroom with a smoky mauve on the walls and a floral headboard.

ABOVE: An arched shower niche provides architectural detail in this new house, where a clawfoot tub feels unexpected.
OPPOSITE: Floral café curtains bring interest to a kids' bathroom.

FOX ISLAND GUEST HOUSE

After we finished the main house on this Fox Island property, the owners asked me to work on the two-bedroom guest house. They are entrepreneurs in the wine business, so they entertain frequently and have family and friends coming and going all the time. The guest house functions like a small home of its own with a fully equipped kitchen and dining and living area.

By the time I was brought onto the job, the architect had finalized the plans for an open-concept living area, a layout I always find tricky. From the front door, you entered into one big space. The design echoed the main house, with the same high ceilings and upper windows. I had learned a few lessons from working with those soaring spaces in the main house and knew that we needed to drop the ceilings in every room, except for the living room. Adding architectural details like arched walls created some natural division between the living, dining, and kitchen areas. That allowed us an opportunity to change the flooring materials and use a mix of wallpaper patterns and paint colors, maintaining the feeling of openness but also a sense of transition from one space to another.

Another challenge to work around was the stone fireplace, which is a little deep for the size of the room and juts out into the small living area. To balance its

Delicately patterned wallpaper pairs with a floating console in walnut burlwood and an Italian mid-century sconce.

TAMSIN JOHNSON *Spaces for Living*

WORKSTEAD INTERIORS OF BEAUTY
AND NECESSITY

scale, we flanked it with two chunky sofas covered in a graphic print and a graceful mohair velvet chair. The fabric lamp shade adds a soft fluidity.

The dining room is a narrow slice in the center of the living area. We made it feel like its own distinct space by using floral wallpaper and a delicate vintage Italian brass chandelier over a modern walnut table and dining chairs upholstered in rose velvet.

Hardwood flooring leads to hexagonal terracotta in the kitchen, which is painted a deep navy blue. The built-in dining nook along that wall is a great example of the mash-up of styles I love, combining rustic terracotta with a Saarinen table, wishbone chairs, and a bench upholstered in a traditional Michael Smith fabric. It's the balance of old and new that is appealing. The lighting in this house is very special, from the wall sconces to the pendants and chandeliers. I was able to use vintage fixtures that I had my eye on for a while, and I knew the clients were adventurous enough to go for them.

The two bedrooms also have a dark, romantic mood. In one room, we covered the walls in navy grass cloth. I designed the camelback headboard. I tend

PREVIOUS SPREAD: We added archways to create separate zones for living and formal dining and an eat-in kitchen. Wallpaper and paneling delineate these spaces further. OPPOSITE: Like the living room in the main house, this room is centered around an imposing stone fireplace. A pair of chunky sofas in a modern blue floral are grounded with a jute rug. FOLLOWING SPREAD: Vintage light fixtures give new construction a layer that is often missing.

to stick with simpler headboard shapes, so this was a bit of a departure, but I liked the undulating form in this room. The plaid fabric is countered by an ornate vintage sconce and a stately old chair in a floral that looks like it could have been grabbed from the corner of a very stylish grandmother's room. The second bedroom has aubergine painted walls, a great spindle bed, and a patterned Chinese rug that's a beautiful alternative to a standard Moroccan.

The tile in the bathroom was imported from Italy, and it's one of the real highlights of this project for me. In the powder room, we used a deep indigo with a black pattern on the walls. It's moody and unique. The marble-top vanity is custom, and the brass sconces are vintage. The second full bath is my favorite bathroom ever. We designed the vanity to feel like a piece of furniture, with delicate legs. A vanity that extends to the floor with a toe-kick isn't always necessary, especially in a guest bath that doesn't require much storage. And the contrast of the off-lilac tile and the red print feels very Northern Italian.

PREVIOUS PAGES: Cloudy gray marble pairs with glossy blue-black paneling and rustic terracotta floor tiles. RIGHT: A curvy headboard in a rag plaid mixes with a vintage sconce.

OPPOSITE AND ABOVE: A unique combination of hand-painted tiles in terracotta with glossy lilac squares in a bathroom.

ABOVE: A layered approach to bedding is a tenet of our work. OPPOSITE: An antique
Chinese rug and rich aubergine walls ground this guest bedroom.

ABOVE: A close-up of the hand-painted Italian tile in the guest house's bathroom reveals the subtle scroll pattern in deep blue.
OPPOSITE: Against the dark tile, the Hans Kögl sconces—a rare find—and a floating wood vanity sing.

COW HOLLOW

One reason I love British design is that it's tailored to a part of the world that isn't known for great weather. People accept the fact that it's going to be gray and drizzling for much of the year, and they design cozy, inviting, layered interiors to counter that dreariness. Because San Francisco—where this traditional family home is located—is often covered in marine fog and is cool for much of the year, it can feel more like England than sunny California. When I met the homeowners, we bonded over our shared love of color and English interiors. They knew instinctively that the bright, neutral, Bohemian look that's so popular in the rest of the state wouldn't feel right in this historic 1911 home, located in the San Francisco neighborhood of Cow Hollow, near the Presidio just south of the marina. Together, we interpreted classic British design in a more modern way.

    We began the design process in the kitchen, which is quite dark and has only a single window that faces a stairwell. There was nothing we could do to the layout to make it lighter because there are houses butting up against two sides of the home—there was simply no place to add a window. The best option was to embrace the low-light atmosphere by painting the walls and cabinet a deep navy and installing a stone floor and soapstone countertops and a custom-fabricated soapstone sink. I wanted it to feel immersive. The island is quite narrow, and we designed it that way so we'd still have enough clearance around it on all sides in

This 1911 San Francisco city house has quirky charm. A table and a pair of skirted chairs greet visitors in the foyer.

the square footprint. There are two layers of lighting, flush mounts and pendants, available when the owners need to brighten up the space for meal preparation. In contrast, the adjacent dining nook features windows on two sides. I love that contrast of light and dark, moving from a shadowy room into a fully lit dining space designed with a built-in bench that has deep drawers for storing linens and dishware underneath.

One of the more unconventional aspects of this home's funky layout is that there is no formal dining room. The clients knew they wouldn't use it, so they opted to create three living rooms with the extra space, two on the main floor and one upstairs adjacent to the bedrooms.

On the main floor, the front door opens onto a foyer with a round table and two chairs. We installed climbing vine wallpaper here, with small birds and flowers, to cover the walls up through the stairwell, creating an interior garden.

Adjacent to the entry is a more casual family area we call the "hearth room." This feels like a classic British room to me, with the small-scale fireplace, muddy brown walls, and a striped Indian dhurrie rug. There's a deck just outside the double French doors at the bay window, so it can get very bright when the sun is out, but most of the time it's cozy. On the opposite side of the entry is the original living room, a long, somewhat narrow space that was an awkward size to furnish. We decided to create two separate conversation areas that are petite in scale. The color combination in this room is bold, with Farrow & Ball's Setting Plaster pink on the walls, upholstered furniture in shades of eggplant and blue, and a deep ruby sofa that's buttoned up and proper.

PREVIOUS PAGES: The foyer and adjacent hearth room, with papered and paneled walls and the vintage-style moldings, look like they belong in a terraced house in Notting Hill. RIGHT: The hearth room has walls in deep brown, a cheerful print on a chair, and a striped rug.

PREVIOUS SPREAD: A sitting room on the second floor features a lively color palette and cozy skirted sofa in a delicate floral. OPPOSITE AND ABOVE: William Morris wallpaper mixes with classic Delft tile, lilac paint, and cherry red accents. FOLLOWING SPREAD: The low-light kitchen was made for dark, moody cabinets and walls.

PREVIOUS PAGES: Blue-black millwork in the kitchen is grounded with antique limestone flooring. OPPOSITE AND ABOVE: A bay window and French doors bathe the dining room nook in light, and provide views out into the yard.

OPPOSITE AND ABOVE: An additional bathroom was carved out of a kids' closet. The vine-pattern wallpaper in the background extends from the ground floor to the top of the stairwell. Leaf-green paint and brass accents pair with a wood vanity.

ABOVE: In the living room, rust-red upholstery and soft blush walls pair well with an antique rug. OPPOSITE: A small conversation area by the fireplace.

ABOVE AND RIGHT: The third-floor attic bedroom has contrasting patterns on walls and ceilings, mixed with a rush headboard and layered rugs.

On the second floor, there is a private living room we call the "lady's den" that serves as a retreat for a busy mother of three. There are cozy chairs for reading, a conversation area, and a small desk. We covered the walls in a William Morris pattern and used Delft tile for the small fireplace. The palette is cheery and feminine. She can close the door and have it all to herself, without a single toy in sight.

I loved designing the boys' rooms upstairs because the clients were open to the idea of using some unexpected color, like the dusty pink draperies and florals. The muted rose color is often perceived as feminine, but I find that when paired with a boxy valance it feels neutral, or even masculine. These rooms give the impression that the house was inherited, as if the kids were occupying bedrooms decorated long ago for a previous generation. Yet they still offer plenty of storage for toys and comfortable spots to play and read, and the boys love their rooms.

I'd been looking for the perfect room in the house to cover in pattern. When I saw the layout of the primary bedroom suite, with all of its nooks and angles, I knew it was the opportunity I'd been waiting for. I used two contrasting wallpaper prints and covered all the surfaces, including the ceiling. The generous use of pattern and layered rugs give this room a rich, eclectic feel. Choosing the mix of patterns was a painstaking process. We wanted to push it without going overboard. It's a delicate balance, but I love how it feels when you walk into that room.

The primary bathroom is narrow so we opted to use paneling on the lower walls and a reclaimed marble checkerboard on the floor. The vanity is designed to look like an old dresser.

PREVIOUS SPREAD: Rose curtains are an unexpected twist in a boys' room. ABOVE: A built-in window seat adds charm to the nursery. OPPOSITE: This floral chair is a favorite spot for bedtime stories.

KENTFIELD

This house in the North Bay, over the Golden Gate Bridge from San Francisco, feels like magic. You can wander through the immense double doors to beautiful gardens and a lovely pool. The property is filled with sunshine. Majestic Mount Tamalpais sits in the background. The home itself is light and airy, with generous skylights and floor-to-ceiling windows. Every time I visit, I have a hard time leaving.

My clients, a young couple, bought this house when they decided to move away from the city. They were first-time home buyers, but they had mature and assured taste. They weren't afraid to make sophisticated choices.

During our early discussions about what they wanted in a home, I noticed that none of the images they presented to me featured any pattern at all. It was clear that they wanted the design to be quintessential California with a British edge. To accomplish this classic-with-a-twist aesthetic, we used pattern in bold ways, but we kept mixed prints to a minimum, which is quieter and more traditional.

The design scheme that we landed on feels like the Bay Area meets the English countryside. The palette is very pale and neutral and features pistachio green, maize yellow, and dusty pink. The walls in the primary bedroom are

Upholstered walls and layers of textiles make a cozy corner in the primary suite.

upholstered in a small-scale print by Penny Morrison, and we played with subtle florals for upholstered pieces and cozy window seats.

This house feels slightly different from my typical work, where I tend to play with asymmetry. I rarely do coordinated sofas or uniform furniture layouts. We made an exception in this house, where twin sofas, a set of rattan chairs, and repetition of textiles felt proper. We had some fun with the powder room, adding a sink skirted in a favorite Michael Smith fabric, block-print wallpaper, a wicker light fixture, and an Italian mid-century brass mirror. Keeping the patterns to a minimum but using them in impactful ways helped achieve the quieter aesthetic these clients desired. The result is timeless and welcoming, and will age through the years with grace.

OPPOSITE: A caned coffee table and antique side table in the formal living room.
FOLLOWING SPREAD: A pair of matching sofas in a restrained floral is offset by an antique Tuareg rug and soft green millwork.

PREVIOUS SPREAD: Natural materials nod to the California landscape. OPPOSITE AND ABOVE: Rush-backed dining chairs upholstered in earthy brown linen mix well with a Swedish console and a modern chandelier.

OPPOSITE: The den is wallpapered in navy grass cloth and has two sofas in a favorite print from Carolina Irving. ABOVE: A skirted sink and sculptural mirror in a powder room are playful but refined. FOLLOWING SPREAD: Simple counter stools and uncluttered surfaces contribute to the serene aesthetic.

OPPOSITE: The primary bedroom has upholstered walls and ceilings in a mid-scale floral.
ABOVE: An extra-deep window seat with a pile of pillows offers a lovely view of Mount Tamalpais.

THE CABIN
AND THE SNUG

After a thorough search for a weekend getaway house across the many tiny islands that are a short ferry ride from our home in Tacoma, we discovered Anderson Island and knew right away that it was our place.

It's the southernmost island in the sound, accessible only by boat, and small, a little less than 8 square miles. It was a seasonal spot for the Nisqually and Steilacoom tribes to harvest berries, find cedar trees to make canoes, and fish for salmon; in the nineteenth century Scandinavian settlers began to arrive. Today there are roughly 1,000 full-time residents. It's the kind of place that stays quiet year-round, where the swimming hole is never crowded, and where you can spend long afternoons looking for crabs and shells along the shore.

We fell in love with a charming house that had much potential, built in 1953 on a long stretch of beach. Our goal was to create a retreat large enough to host three families for a weekend, and to make it our own without sacrificing too many of its original details, like built-in shelving and storage, and a simple brick fireplace. It's all wood inside, with warm plank floors and oak-paneled walls that we painted a deep blue-black. We updated the kitchen with brass fixtures and wood countertops and transformed a laundry room into a bunk room for our twin sons. We also took over a rarely used garage to create a two-bedroom guest house that we refer to as "the Snug."

Even though the cabin makes us feel completely removed from the distractions of daily life, it takes us no time at all to get there. It's about forty-five minutes door-to-door, but it's an entire world away. It's a gathering place for us, and for our friends, and a wonderful place to make memories.

The spindle-leg console, topped with a vintage yellow lamp with an Ian Sanderson fabric shade, is a spot to stash books and bags.

PREVIOUS SPREAD: Down Pipe by Farrow & Ball is a great color for a seaside cabin in the misty Northwest. It looks charcoal gray on dark days and almost navy in sunlight. ABOVE AND OPPOSITE: Nautical paintings nod to the location on the water, while plaid chairs provide contrast to the saffron sofa. FOLLOWING PAGE LEFT: The original millwork was left intact and painted to match the walls. FOLLOWING PAGE RIGHT: Bare wood floors, a rustic farm table, vintage wood chairs, and a Noguchi lantern in the dining room.

OPPOSITE: A corner of the living room with a vintage rattan daybed is a favorite spot to curl up and enjoy the view.
ABOVE: A breakfast nook was added for cozy cabin mornings.

PREVIOUS PAGES: The bedrooms are painted a forest green and are filled with vintage furniture and accessories I've collected over the years. ABOVE: In a guest bathroom, antique sconces and a rope mirror have a nautical feel. OPPOSITE: A vintage wicker sofa with mismatched textiles creates the perfect vibe for lazy, off-grid weekends.

ABOVE AND OPPOSITE: In a cozy bunk room, a simple cotton rag rug, plaid shams, and ticking stripe quilts evoke classic Americana style.

ON COLLABORATION
(AND MEMORIES OF HOME)

Heidi and I got lucky when we found each other almost eight years ago. We just clicked, right from the start, and we've had an incredible partnership since. We trusted each other from the very beginning and found shared comfort. Simply put, home is a place that makes everyone comfortable, and Heidi understands that in a deep, almost maternal way. When I'm in a home that she designed, it always reminds me of my mother, even though as a child I didn't experience anything like the homes we photograph.

Everyone wants to curl up and live in these photos, in the spaces she creates, including me.

When I was a child, I lived in immigration camps.

I'm from Bosnia. When the war started, my dad stayed behind and fought, and my mother and I left our home. We ended up in Jordan in the refugee system, and home for me was a big, open room shared by two families with only a pink drape hung between them. I didn't see my father for many years. From the time I was ten years old, my escape was creativity. It was books, photos, magazines, and my imagination. I ended up in this field because I seek the comfort of home through imagining in and creating spaces. And to this day I try to give that same feeling to others.

When we met, we had an appointment at a little local restaurant in Seattle, the way people do when they're trying to get to know each other. We were a little nervous and asked all the typical questions: *How do you do this? How do you do that?* It was obvious that we had a similar sensibility, but ultimately, we connected because of our humor. We're very similar that way. We have a high level of commitment, a desire to get things done, but we are always laughing together.

Working as we do in someone's home can be a stressful situation. There's art falling off temporary hooks on the walls. We're moving things around. We're a little on edge, because it can feel so invasive. We tiptoe through that space together, trying always to remain respectful. I remember one shoot in Colorado when we lost our minds from altitude sickness. It was the middle of the night, and Heidi knocked on my hotel room door. She said, "I'm itchy and loopy and I can't sleep," and I felt the same way. Still, we couldn't stop laughing. It was weird and hilarious. And we got up early the next day and powered through.

Heidi and I often talk about the moment when her work shifted and her palette got darker. At the time, interior photography was bright, blown out, and oversaturated. Moodier photos with low light were not yet a thing. I shot her work in a darker, different way. When we looked at those muddier photos together, something clicked, and Heidi left behind her Californian aesthetic and tapped into something that felt a little masculine, that played on that mix of girlish and manly, using more saturated colors like moody purples and marshy greens to balance the florals she had always favored. It was a look that appealed to every member of the family, regardless of gender. There's a disarming factor to her work—it takes everyone by surprise.

Make it cozy. That was the mission. And we really connected from that place.

Our connection is also based around our memories of home, and our shared desire to make every space we live in feel like home. As children, we both moved frequently and didn't experience stability or the kind of grounded, balanced environments Heidi creates.

To give someone a sense of home is very important to both me and Heidi. Our shared vision and our shared trust made this possible. It's such an honor to put this work out into the world.

—Haris Kenjar

ACKNOWLEDGMENTS

First and foremost, to my husband, Justin. You have been a steady and constant source of strength as I have navigated this career path and its many ups and downs. You have taken on the workload of nearly everything else in our lives to allow me the space and freedom to follow my passion. Our life together is the dream come true.

To my wonderful team who make it all possible, and who approach every day with positivity and enthusiasm (no small feat!): Kate Livsey, Anna Forrester, and Maloree McCormick. You all buoy me and keep me wonderfully excited about the future. Thank you.

Thank you to Christine Lennon for your beautiful words.

To Doug Turshen and David Huang for your collaboration and willingness to work together to create this book. I'm still pinching myself that it's mine.

To my editor, Kathleen Jayes, and the whole team at Rizzoli for believing in my work and the concept for this book. It has been the honor of a lifetime.

Jenny Pfeffer, who expertly captured the concept for this book in one go and guided me to find the right home for it.

Many thanks to James Mobley for the beautiful artwork on these end pages. And to Amber Lewis for the kind words.

And to Haris, who has been by my side since the beginning (or at least what I think of as the beginning). I do not think every designer is lucky enough to find a collaborator who not only deeply understands their vision and can bring it to life, but also feels like family. Our relationship has been one of the great joys of my life. None of this would be possible without you.

This industry is deep and complex and I appreciate the makers, craftspeople, and vendors who support designers, making our work possible. We cannot create these homes in a vacuum. They are living things that require hundreds, sometimes thousands, of hands to bring them to life. I'm indebted to all of you.

I'm constantly astounded by the beauty, generosity, and creativity in this field. I have found the most supportive community in so many of you. I think many believe this industry is shrouded in trade secrets and mystery, but I have found the opposite to be true.

Finally, to our clients—the work is not possible without your trust. It is such an honor to bring these homes to life, and to craft spaces for you to create memories with your families.

—Heidi

First published in the United States of America in 2023 by
Rizzoli International Publications, Inc.
300 Park Avenue South
New York, NY 10010
www.rizzoliusa.com

Photography: Haris Kenjar
Foreword: Amber Lewis
Text: Christine Lennon

Publisher: Charles Miers
Senior Editor: Kathleen Jayes
Design: Doug Turshen with David Huang
Production Manager: Barbara Sadick
Managing Editor: Lynn Scrabis

Printed in Singapore

2023 2024 2025 2026 / 10 9 8 7 6 5 4 3 2 1

ISBN: 978-0-8478-7347-0

Library of Congress Control Number: 2023934171

Visit us online:
Facebook.com/RizzoliNewYork
Twitter: @Rizzoli_Books
Instagram.com/RizzoliBooks
Pinterest.com/RizzoliBooks
Youtube.com/user/RizzoliNY
Issuu.com/Rizzoli